# Welcome to Iceland

### By Ben Hubbard

**Senior Editors** Carrie Love, Shannon Beatty
**Assistant Editor** Gunjan Mewati
**Senior Art Editor** Rachael Parfitt
**Art Editor** Bhagyashree Nayak
**Assistant Art Editor** Simran Lakhiani
**Jacket Coordinator** Issy Walsh
**Jacket Designer** Dheeraj Arora
**DTP Designers** Vikram Singh, Sachin Gupta
**Picture Researchers** Rituraj Singh, Sumedha Chopra
**Production Editor** Abi Maxwell
**Production Controller** John Casey
**Managing Editors** Penny Smith, Monica Saigal
**Managing Art Editor** Ivy Sengupta
**Delhi Creative Heads** Glenda Fernandes, Malavika Talukder
**Publishing Manager** Francesca Young
**Deputy Art Director** Mabel Chan
**Publishing Director** Sarah Larter

**Reading Consultant** Dr. Barbara Marinak
**Subject Consultant** Angus Konstam

First American Edition, 2021
Published in the United States by DK Publishing
1450 Broadway, Suite 801, New York, NY 10018

DK books are available at special discounts when purchased
in bulk for sales promotions, premiums, fund-raising, or
educational use. For details, contact: DK Publishing Special Markets,
1450 Broadway, Suite 801, New York, NY 10018
SpecialSales@dk.com

Printed and bound in China

The publisher would like to thank the following for their kind permission to reproduce their photographs:
(Key: a-above; b-below/bottom; c-center; f-far; l-left; r-right; t-top)
**1 Alamy Stock Photo:** Juniors Bildarchiv GmbH (b). **5 Getty Images / iStock:** patpongs. **6–7 Dreamstime.com:**
Jon Helgason (b). **7 Alamy Stock Photo:** Arterra Picture Library (c). **8 Getty Images / iStock:** DieterMeyrl.
**9 Alamy Stock Photo:** Peter Barritt. **10–11 Alamy Stock Photo:** Juniors Bildarchiv GmbH. **12 Dreamstime.com:**
Henkbogaard (t). **Getty Images / iStock:** Mizuki Kato (b). **13 Dreamstime.com:** Lecock Freddy. **14 Dreamstime.com:**
Peter Hermes Furian (t). **14–15 Shutterstock.com:** SAPhotog (t). **16 Dreamstime.com:** Mypointofview (cb).
**Getty Images / iStock:** pedrojperez (br). **17 Getty Images / iStock:** Snorri Guðmundsson (c). **18 Dreamstime.com:**
Artofphoto. **19 Getty Images:** Simon Hofmann / Bongarts. **20–21 Dreamstime.com:** Tawatchai Prakobkit.
**22 Dreamstime.com:** Tawatchai Prakobkit (bl); Pytyczech (tl); Tampaci (cla); Robin Runck (cl).
**Getty Images:** Simon Hofmann / Bongarts (clb).

**Cover images:** *Front:* **Dreamstime.com:** Suranga Weeratunga; *Back:* **Dreamstime.com:** Marek Rybar tl.

**Endpaper images:** *Front:* **Dreamstime.com:** Sandy Matzen; *Back:* **Dreamstime.com:** Sandy Matzen.

All other images © Dorling Kindersley
For further information see: www.dkimages.com

**For the curious**
**www.dk.com**

MIX
Paper from
responsible sources
**FSC** **FSC™ C018179**
www.fsc.org

This book was made with Forest
Stewardship Council™ certified paper—
one small step in DK's commitment to
a sustainable future. For more information
go to www.dk.com/our-green-pledge

# Contents

# Where is Iceland?

Iceland is a country in Europe.
It is an island in the Atlantic Ocean.
The capital city is Reykjavik (RAKE-ya-veek).

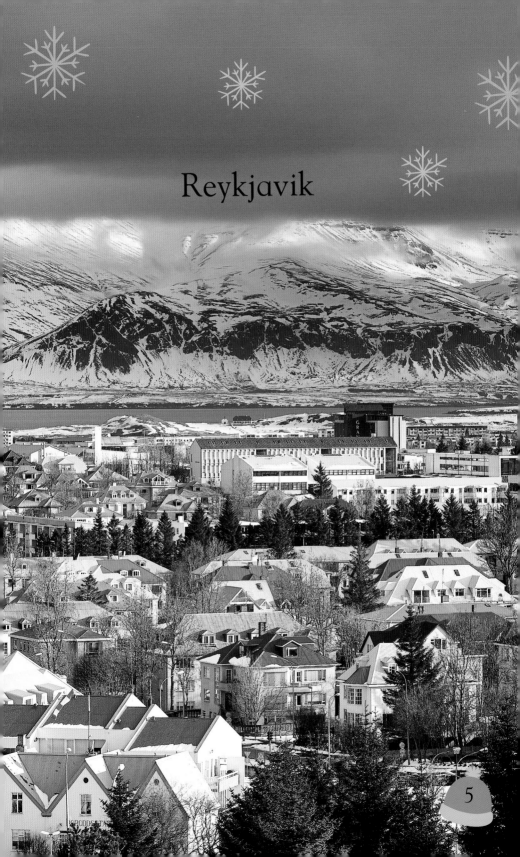

Reykjavik

# Fire and ice

An ice cap is a
thick mass of snow.
Areas of Iceland are
covered by ice caps.

# Iceland has 130 volcanoes.

# Hot springs

Iceland is covered
in natural hot springs.
The water is heated
by hot rocks.
People swim in the springs.

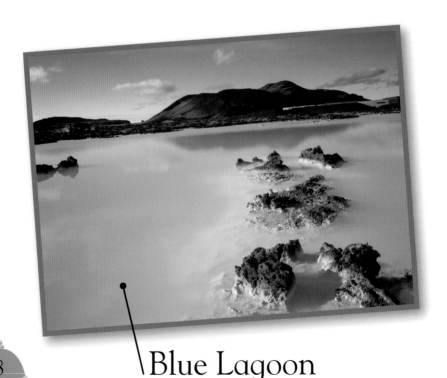

Blue Lagoon

# Icelandic horses

The Icelandic horse is small and strong.

It has a thick coat to stay
warm in the snow.

# Puffins

The puffin is a small seabird.
It can fly and swim.
There are almost 10 million
puffins in Iceland.

Puffin
chick

# Vikings

The Vikings discovered Iceland. They settled there over 1,000 years ago.

Viking longhouse

They lived together in longhouses.

# Food

People eat lamb soup, hotdogs, and shark meat.

Lamb soup

Hotdog

Skyr

They eat yogurt for dessert.
It's called skyr (s-KEER).

# Sports

People climb mountains
in Iceland.
Handball is popular too.

# Northern lights

You can see the northern
lights in Iceland.

These are natural lights
in the sky.

# Glossary

**Europe**
continent with
over 50 countries

**handball**
sport played by two
teams using a small ball

**hot spring**
pool of warm water that
is heated by hot rocks

**ice cap**
thick mass of
ice and snow

**Northern lights**
natural light display
seen near the Arctic

# Index

## A LEVEL FOR EVERY READER

This book is a part of an exciting four-level reading series to support children in developing the habit of reading widely for both pleasure and information. Each book is designed to develop a child's reading skills, fluency, grammar awareness, and comprehension in order to build confidence and enjoyment when reading.

### Ready for a Level 1 (Learning to Read) book

A child should:

- be familiar with most letters and sounds.
- understand how to blend sounds together to make words.
- have an awareness of syllables and rhyming sounds.

### A valuable and shared reading experience

For many children, learning to read requires much effort, but adult participation can make reading both fun and easier. Here are a few tips on how to use this book with an early reader:

*Check out the contents together:*

- tell the child the book title and talk about what the book might be about.
- read about the book on the back cover and talk about the contents page to help heighten interest and expectation.
- chat about the pictures on each page.
- discuss new or difficult words.

*Support the reader:*

- give the book to the young reader to turn the pages.
- if the book seems too hard, support the child by sharing the reading task.

*Talk at the end of each page:*

- ask questions about the text and the meaning of the words used—this helps develop comprehension skills.

Reading consultant: Dr. Barbara Marinak, Dean and Professor of Education at Mount St. Mary's University, Maryland.

24